THE HOUND OF HEAVEN

THE HOUND OF HEAVEN
By FRANCIS THOMPSON

NEW YORK
DODD, MEAD AND COMPANY
1922

Garrett Biblical Institute
Evanston, Illinois

INTRODUCTION

The Rev. Mark J. McNeal. S. J., who was one of the successors of Lafcadio Hearn in the chair of English Literature at the Tokyo Imperial University, in an interesting article recounts the following incident of his experience in that institution. "I was seated on the examining board with Professor Ichikawa, the dean of the English department . . . There entered the room a student whom I recognized as among the best in the class, a sharp young chap with big Mongolian eyes, and one who had never to my knowledge given any hint of even a leaning toward Christianity. I remembered, however, that his thesis submitted for a degree had been a study of Francis Thompson. Following the usual custom, I began to question him about his thesis.

" 'Why did you choose Thompson?'

" 'Well, he is quite a famous poet.'

INTRODUCTION

" 'What kind of poet is he?'

" 'We might call him a mystic.'

" 'Is he a mystic of the orthodox sort, like Cynewulf or Crashaw; or an unorthodox mystic, like Blake or Shelley?'

" 'Oh, he's orthodox.'

" 'Well, now, what do you consider his greatest production?'

" 'Why, I should say "The Hound of Heaven." '

" 'Well, what on earth does Thompson mean by that Hound?'

" 'He means God.'

" 'But is not that a rather irreverent way for Thompson to be talking about God, calling Him a hound? What does he mean by comparing God to a hound?'

" 'Well, he means the pursuit of God.'

" 'Oh, I see, Thompson is pursuing God, is he?'

" 'Oh, no. He is rather running away from God.'

" 'Well, then, God is pursuing Thompson, is that it?'

" 'Yes, that's it.'

INTRODUCTION

" 'But, see here; according to Thompson's belief God is everywhere, isn't He?'

" 'Yes.'

" 'Well, then, how can God be going after Thompson? Is it a physical pursuit?'

" 'No. It is a moral pursuit.'

" 'A moral pursuit! What's that? What is God after?'

" 'He is after Thompson's love.'

"And then we, the Jesuit and the Buddhist, began to follow the windings and turnings of that wondrous poem, the most mystic and spiritual thing that has been written since St. Teresa laid down her pen. What the other member of the examining board thought of it all I never heard. But I think I acquired a satisfactory answer to that question so often put to me: Can the Japanese really grasp a spiritual truth? Do they really get at the meaning of Christianity? This, of a race that has produced more martyrs than any other nation since the fall of Rome and that kept the Faith for two centuries without a visible symbol or document!"

INTRODUCTION

The incident supplies matter for other conclu-
sions more germane to the subject of this essay.
The late Bert Leston Taylor, a journalist whose
journalism had a literary facet of critical bril-
liance, once declared that he could not perceive the
excellence of Francis Thompson's poetry. When
someone suggested that it might be that he was not
spiritual enough, the retort was laconic and crushing, "Or, perhaps, not ecclesiastical enough."
Like most good retorts Taylor's had more wit than
truth. He was obsessed by the notion, prevalent
among a certain class of literary critics, that Francis Thompson's fame was the artificially stimu-
lated applause of a Catholic coterie, whose enthu-
siasm could hardly be shared by readers with no
particular curiosity about Catholic ideas or modes
of religion. It was probably this obsession which
prompted that able critic, Mr. H. D. Traill, to
write to Mr. Wilfrid Meynell when the "Hound
of Heaven" first appeared: "I quite agree with
you in thinking him a remarkable poet, but, if he
is ever to become other than a 'poet's poet' or
'critic's poet'—if indeed it is worth anyone's am-

bition to be other than that—it will only be by working in a different manner. A 'public' to appreciate the 'Hound of Heaven' is to me inconceivable." Mr. William Archer, an experienced judge of popular likes, was of the same opinion. "Yet," Francis Thompson's biographer tells us, "in the three years after Thompson's death the separate edition of the 'Hound of Heaven' sold fifty thousand copies; and, apart from anthologies, many more thousands were sold of the books containing it." When the "Hound of Heaven" is selected for study, and explained in words of one syllable, by a young Japanese student in the Tokyo Imperial University almost thirty years after the poem was published, one can hardly maintain that it calls for certain ecclesiastical affiliations before it can be understood and felt, or that its "public" is necessarily circumscribed.

It must be owned, indeed that Francis Thompson was a puzzle to his contemporaries of the nineties. He paid the usual penalty of vaulting originality. The decade is famous for its bold experiments and shining successes in the art of poetry.

INTRODUCTION

One might expect that a public, grown accustomed to exquisitely wrought novelties and eager to extend them a welcome, would have been preordained to recognize and hail the genius of Thompson. But it was not so. The estheticism of the nineties, for all its sweet and fragile flowers, was rooted in the dark passions of the flesh. Its language was the language of death and despair and annihilation and the Epicurean need of exhausting the hedonistic possibilities of life ere the final engulfing in darkness and silence. When the speech of Thompson, laden with religion and spirituality and Christian mystery, broke with golden turbulence upon the world of the nineties, the critics were abashed and knew not what to think of it. The effect was somewhat like that produced by Attwater, in Stevenson's "The Ebb-Tide," when he began suddenly to discourse on Divine Grace to the amazement of Herrick and his crew of scoundrels from the stolen *Farallone*. "Oh," exclaimed the unspeakable Huish, when they had recovered breath, "Oh, look 'ere, turn down the lights at once, and the Band of 'Ope will oblige! This ain't a

10

spiritual séance." It had something akin to the madness of poor Christopher Smart when he fell into the habit of dropping on his knees and praying in the crowded London streets. There was incongruity, verging on the indecent, in this intrusion of religion into art, as if an archangel were to attend an afternoon tea in Mayfair or an absinthe session in a Bohemian café. It was, in Dr. Johnson's phrase, "an unnecessary deviation from the usual modes of the world" which struck the world dumb.

The poetry of Francis Thompson appeared in three small volumes: "Poems," published in 1893; "Sister Songs," in 1895; and "New Poems," in 1897. The first of these volumes contained the "Hound of Heaven"; though it staggered reviewers at large, they yielded dubious and carefully measured praise and waited for developments. The pack was unleashed and the hue-and-cry raised on the coming of "Sister Songs" and "New Poems." Andrew Lang and Mr. Arthur Symons led the chorus of disapproval. It is amusing to read now that Francis Thompson's "faults are fundamental. Though he uses the treasure of the Temple, he is not a religious poet. The note of a true spiritual passion never once sounds in his book." Another critic of the poet declares that "nothing could be stronger than his language, nothing weaker than the impression it leaves on the mind. It is like a dictionary of obsolete English suffering from a severe fit of delirium tremens." A prominent literary periodical saw, in the attempt to foist Thompson on the public as a genuine poet, a sectarian effort to undermine the literary press of England. In the course of a year the sale of "Sister Songs" amounted to 349 copies. The "New Poems" fared worse; its sale, never large, practically ceased a few years after its appearance, three copies being sold during the first six months of 1902.

And all this despite strong recommendations from fastidious quarters. George Meredith's recognition was instantaneous and unreserved. Henley's was accompanied by reproofs. Mr. Richard LeGallienne was enthusiastic. Mr. William Archer said to a friend, "This is not work which can possibly be *popular* in the wide sense; but it is work that will be read and treasured centuries hence by those who really care for poetry." And he wrote to Thompson, "I assure you no conceivable reaction can wipe out or overlay such work as yours. It is firm-based on the rock of absolute beauty; and this I say all the more confidently because it does not happen to appeal to my own speculative, or even my own literary, prejudices." The most extravagant admirer of all, and the one who will probably turn out to have come nearer the mark than any of Francis Thompson's contemporaries, was Mr. J. L. Garvin, the well known English leader-writer in politics and literature. "After the publication of his second volume," he wrote in the English *Bookman*, March 1897, "when it became clear that the 'Hound of Heaven' and 'Sister Songs' should be read together as a strict lyrical sequence, there was no longer any comparison possible except the highest, the inevitable comparison with even Shakespeare's Sonnets. The Sonnets are the greatest soliloquy in literature. The 'Hound of Heaven' and 'Sister Songs' are the second greatest; and there is no third. In each case it is rather consciousness imaged in the magic mirror of poetry than explicit autobiography. . . . Even with the greatest pages of 'Sister Songs' sounding in one's ears, one is sometimes tempted to think the 'Hound of Heaven' Mr. Thompson's high-water mark for unimaginable beauty and tremendous import—if we do damnably iterate Mr. Thompson's tremendousness, we cannot help it, he thrusts the word upon us. We do not think we forget any of the splendid things of an English anthology when we say that the 'Hound of Heaven' seems to us, on the whole, the most wonderful lyric (if we consider 'Sister Songs' as a sequence of lyrics) in the language. It fingers all the stops of the spirit, and we hear now a thrilling and dolorous note of doom and now the quiring of the spheres and now the very pipes of Pan, but under all the still sad music of humanity. It is the return of the nineteenth century to Thomas à Kempis. . . . The regal air, the prophetic ardors, the apocalyptic vision, Mr. Thompson has them all. A rarer, more intense, more strictly predestinate genius has never been known to poetry. To many this will seem the simple delirium of over-emphasis. The writer signs for those others, nowise ashamed, who range after Shakespeare's very Sonnets the poetry of a living poet, Francis Thompson."

We do not associate Mr. Arnold Bennett with any of the ideas in religion or literature which supplied impulse to Francis Thompson. It is a surprise of the first magnitude to find him carried away into the rapture of prophecy by the "Sister Songs." "I declare," he says in an article appearing in July, 1895, "that for three days after this book appeared I read nothing else. I went about repeating snatches of it—snatches such as—

'The innocent moon, that nothing does but shine,
Moves all the labouring surges of the world.'

My belief is that Francis Thompson has a richer natural genius, a finer poetical equipment, than any poet save Shakespeare. Show me the divinest glories of Shelley and Keats, even of Tennyson, who wrote the 'Lotus Eaters' and the songs in the 'Princess,' and I think I can match them all out of this one book, this little book that can be bought at an ordinary bookseller's shop for an ordinary prosaic crown. I fear that in thus extolling Francis Thompson's work, I am grossly outraging the canons of criticism. For the man is alive, he gets up of a morning like common mortals, not improbably he eats bacon for breakfast; and every critic with an atom of discretion knows that a poet must not be called great until he is dead or very old. Well, please yourself what you think. But, in time to come, don't say I didn't tell you." A whole generation of men has passed away since these words appeared; but they do not seem to be so fantastic and whimsical now as they seemed to be then.

It can scarcely be claimed that the prophecies of Meredith, Mr. Garvin, and Mr. Arnold Bennett were of the kind which ultimately assures the event. The reading-world dipped curiously into the pages about which there was so much conflict of opinion; it was startled and bewildered by a novel and difficult form of verse; and finally it agreed with the majority of critics that it was mostly nonsense—too Catholic to be catholic. The poems sold badly, the 'Hound of Heaven' faring best. It is a common mark of genius to be ahead of its time. Even Thompson's coreligionists were cold. Indeed, it may be said they were the coldest. If the general reading-public of the nineties suspected Thompson of being a Victorian reactionary of ultramontane mould, the Catholic public feared him for his art. It was a wild unfettered thing which took strange liberties with Catholic pieties and could not be trusted to run in divine grooves. One can afford to extenuate the attitude of reserve. It was a period when brilliant heterodoxies and flaunting decadence were in the air. The fact is, that critics and public delivered Thompson over to the Catholics; and the Catholics would have nothing to do with him. Canon Sheehan could write of Thompson in 1898: "Only two Catholics—literary Catholics—have noticed this surprising genius—Coventry Patmore and Wilfrid Meynell. The vast bulk of our coreligionists have not even heard his name, although it is already bruited amongst the Im-

mortals; and *the* great Catholic poet, for whose
advent we have been straining our vision, has
passed beneath our eyes, sung his immortal songs,
and vanished." This was written almost ten years
before Thompson died, but after his resolve to
write no more poetry.

It is easily within the probabilities that, small
as was Thompson's audience during his lifetime,
it would have been still smaller but for the ex-
traneous interest excited by the strange story of
his life. He was born on December 16, 1859,
in Preston, Lancashire, whence he went at the age
of eleven to Ushaw College, a Catholic boarding
school for boys. This is the college where Lafcadio Hearn received his education; he had left
the school a year or two before young Thompson's arrival. Both boys were designed for the
priesthood. Hearn lost his faith then or shortly
afterwards: Thompson's irregular habits of
dreamy abstraction rendered him unfit for a sac-
erdotal career. When he had completed his
course at college, where he had distinguished
himself in English composition and attained re-

spectable standing in the classics, his father, a hard-working physician, entered the lad, now eighteen, as a student of medicine in Owen College, Manchester. The Thompson family had moved from Preston to Ashton-under-Lyne, where proximity to Manchester made it possible for the young medical student to spend his nights at home.

Francis was of the silent and secretive sort where he could not hope to find intelligent sympathy. This, and some cloudy compromise with his sense of filial dutifulness, will perhaps explain why he passed six years as a student of medicine without any serious purpose of becoming a physician and without informing his father of his disinclination. Three examinations and three failures at intervals of a year were necessary to convince the father of the true state of affairs. Stern measures were adopted; and, although the consequences were pitifully tragical, it is hard to blame the father of Francis. How are we to discover the extraordinary seal in a case that requires special and extraordinary treatment?

Francis was twenty-four years old with no more idea than a child's of how life is planned on practical lines of prosperity. The senior Thompson thought it time for him to learn and issued orders to find employment of some remunerative kind. Accordingly during the next two years Francis served indifferently for brief periods as a clerk in the shop of a maker of surgical instruments and as a canvasser of an encyclopedia. Both experiments in the art of making a living were failures, increasing paternal dissatisfaction. The desperate young man then enlisted in the army, and after a few weeks' of drilling was rejected on the score of physical weakness.

During these shiftless and unhappy years as a listless medical student and laggard apprentice the poet's chief solace was the public library of Manchester. In his daily absences from home his misery suggested another solace of a sinister kind. After a severe illness during his second year of medicine his mother, says his biographer, presented him with a copy of De Quincey's "Confessions of an Opium Eater." It is incredible that a *helluo librorum*, like Thompson, should have reached the age of twenty without ever having read a book which is one of the first to attract every bright school-boy. This would be particularly true of a school-boy who lived near Manchester, De Quincey's own town. But the evidence seems to be against probabilities. Thompson succumbed completely to the influence of the great genius whose temper and circumstances of life were singularly like his own. Experiments in laudanum were made and habits contracted which accentuated a natural unfitness to wrestle with the practical problems of getting on and rendered family intercourse drearier than ever.

In 1885, when he was twenty-six years old, Francis decided to leave home. After a week in Manchester he requested and received from his father the price of a railway ticket for London. The trip to the vast and strange city must have been made with only the vaguest of plans for the future. The despairing youth seemed to have no other purpose than to rid his father of his vexatious presence. There were friends in London, on one of whom Francis was directed to call for a weekly allowance from home. But a temperamental reluctance kept the young man away from those who could help him, and even the weekly allowance after a while came to be unclaimed. The rough, cyclonic forces of the huge city caught this helpless child of a man's years in the full swing of their blind sweep and played sad tricks with him. In a period extending over nearly three years Francis Thompson led the life of a vagrant in the streets and alleys. He made one or two brave essays at regular work of the most commonplace character, but without success. The worn copies of Æschylus and Blake in the pockets of this ragged and gaunt roustabout contained no useful hints for the difficulties of the peculiar situation; its harshness could be transmuted into temporary and blessed oblivion by a drug whenever the means for purchase could be acquired. The Guildhall Library was much frequented until shabbiness was excluded by the policeman. This outcast poet, approaching

22

thirty years of age, was at various times a boot-black, a newsboy, a vendor of matches, a nocturnal denizen of wharves and lounger on the benches of city-parks. His cough-racked frame was the exposed target of cold and rain and winds. He became used to hunger. At one time a sixpence, for holding a horse, was his only earnings for a week. It was while he was aimlessly roaming the streets one night almost delirious from starvation that a prosperous shoe-merchant, benevolently engaged in religious rescue-work, came across Thompson, and, struck by the incongruity of his gentle speech, induced him to accept employment in his shop. But one cannot allow business to suffer on account of an inveterate blunderer, even though the blunderer wear wings and has endeared himself to the family. Mr. McMaster, kindly Anglican lay-missionary, who deserves grateful remembrance for recognizing and temporarily helping merit under the most deceptive disguise, was obliged much against his inclination to dismiss Francis and to allow him to fall back into the pit of squalor and vagabondage.

But the few months of reprieve had supplied Thompson with the impulse to write. Shortly after he was dropped from the McMaster establishment Mr. Wilfrid Meynell, the editor of *Merry England*, a Catholic magazine, received the following letter: "*Feb. 23rd, '87*—Dear Sir,—In enclosing the accompanying article for your inspection, I must ask pardon for the soiled state of the manuscript. It is due, not to slovenliness, but to the strange places and circumstances under which it has been written. For me, no less than Parolles, the dirty nurse experience has something fouled. I enclose stamped envelope for a reply, since I do not desire the return of the manuscript, regarding your judgment of its worthlessness as quite final. I can hardly expect that where my prose fails my verse will succeed. Nevertheless, on the principle of 'Yet will I try the last,' I have added a few specimens of it, with the off chance that one may be less poor than the rest. Apologizing very sincerely for any intrusion on your valuable time, I remain yours with little hope,

"Francis Thompson.

24

INTRODUCTION

"Kindly address your rejection to the Charing Cross Post Office."

The unpromising aspect of the manuscript, thus introduced, was the occasion of editorial neglect for some months. When at last Mr. Meynell gave it his attention he was electrified into action. He wrote to the address given by Thompson. The letter was returned from the dead-letter office after many days. Then he published one of the poems mentioned in the letter, "The Passion of Mary," in the hope that the author would disclose his whereabouts. The plan succeeded and brought a letter from Thompson with a new address. Mr. Meynell tried to waylay him at the new address, a chemist's shop in Drury Lane, but with characteristic shiftlessness the poet forgot to call there for possible letters. But the seller of drugs finally established communications between the editor and the poet, and one day, more than a year after Thompson's first literary venture had been sent, he visited the office of *Merry England*. Mr. Everard Meynell, the poet's biographer, thus describes the entrance of the poet into his father's sanctum. "My father was told that Mr. Thompson wished to see him. 'Show him up,' he said, and was left alone. Then the door opened, and a strange hand was thrust in. The door closed, but Thompson had not entered. Again it opened, again it shut. At the third attempt a waif of a man came in. No such figure had been looked for; more ragged and unkempt than the average beggar, with no shirt beneath his coat and bare feet in broken shoes, he found my father at a loss for words. 'You must have had access to many books when you wrote that essay,' was what he said. 'That,' said Thompson, his shyness at once replaced by an acerbity that afterwards became one of the most familiar of his never-to-be-resented mannerisms, 'that is precisely where the essay fails. I had no books by me at the time save Æschylus and Blake.' There was little to·be done for him at that interview save the extraction of a promise to call again. He made none of the confidences characteristic of a man seeking sympathy and alms. He was secretive and with no eagerness for plans for his benefit, and refused the offer of a small weekly sum that would enable him to sleep in a bed and sit at a table."

By patience and delicately offered kindnesses Mr. and Mrs. Meynell at length won the difficult privilege of helping the shy, nervous, high-strung spirit wandering in pain, hunger and exile amid the indecencies of extreme penury in a great city. They were helped by the friendly sympathy and care of Premonstratensian and Franciscan monks. Thompson had sounded, and become familiar with, the depths of social degradation in all its external aspects of sordidness. The most extraordinary part of his singular experience is that he affords a striking instance of the triumph of soul and mind over beleaguering circumstance. The nightmare of his environment failed to subdue him. He preserved his spiritual sensitiveness, and literary ideals of a most exalted kind, through the most depressing and demoralizing experiences. The following passage in that first essay offered to Mr. Meynell, entitled "Paganism: Old and New," a vindication of Christian over pagan ideals in art, shows the rich, colorful tone of mind of one who could walk unstained among the world's impurities. "Bring back then, I say, in conclusion, even the best age of Paganism, and you smite beauty on the cheek. But you *cannot* bring back the best age of Paganism, the age when Paganism was a faith. None will again behold Apollo in the forefront of the morning, or see Aphrodite in the upper air loose the long lustre of her golden locks. But you *may* bring back—*dii avertant omen*—the Paganism of the days of Pliny, and Statius, and Juvenal; of much philosophy, and little belief; of superb villas and superb taste; of banquets for the palate in the shape of cookery, and banquets for the eye in the shape of art; of poetry singing dead songs on dead themes with the most polished and artistic vocalisation; of everything most polished, from the manners to the marble floors; of vice carefully drained out of sight, and large fountains of virtue springing in the open air;—in one word, a most shining Paganism indeed—as putrescence also shines." Unlike George Gissing and so many others who had to wade to celebrity through sloughs of bitter destitution, Francis Thompson felt no inclination to capitalize his expert knowledge of back streets and alleys for profit and the morbid entertainment of the curious. His single failing in yielding to the attraction of an insidious drug seemed to be impotent to affect his high admirations and his clear perceptions in the regions of honor and religion.

It is surely one of the literary glories of a distinguished family that Mr. and Mrs. Meynell succeeded in helping Thompson to emancipate himself from the enslavement of a tyrannic habit. His poetic genius began to flower in the new liberty. For the next ten years interest in his poetry and literary friends and connections, few and select, made his life comparatively happy. But he maintained a large measure of independence to the last. That he was never ungrateful to those who befriended him, his poems are ample proof. But in London he always had his own lodgings in a cheap but respectable quarter of the city. His unpunctual and preoccupied manner sometimes created small distresses for his devoted friends to relieve. During the last ten years of his life he wrote little poetry. His vitality, never vigorous, was ebbing and unequal to the demands of inspired verse. But during these years of decline he wrote much golden prose. He was a regular and highly valued contibutor to the *Academy*, the *Athenæum*, the *Nation*, and the *Daily Chronicle*. One can hardly fail to be impressed by the mere industry of a writer of reputed slack habits of work. The published volume of his selected essays is literary criticism, as learned and allusive as Matthew Arnold's, and as nicely poised, with the advantage of being poised in more. rarified heights than Arnold's wings could hope to scale. In this book is his classic and most wonderful essay on Shelley, written before his strength began to flag, in which prose seems to be carried off its feet, as it were, in a very storm of poetic impulse. The published essays are not a tithe of Thompson's writings for the press. Moreover, we have a study of Blessed John de la Salle, a little volume on "Health and Holiness," and a large "Life of St. Ignatius Loyola," none of them suggesting even remotely the plantigrade writing of the mechanical hack.

During the last year of his life, when consumption had almost completely undermined resistance, his old habit reasserted its empire. But it was not for long, and can hardly be said to have hastened the end, which came on November 13, 1907, in the Hospital of St. John and St. Elizabeth. He was buried in St. Mary's Cemetery, Kensal Green, and on his coffin were roses from George Meredith's garden, with the poet-novelist's message: "A true poet, one of the small band."

The "Hound of Heaven" has been called the greatest ode in the English language. Such was the contemporary verdict of some of the most respected critics of the time, and the conviction of its justness deepens with the passing of years. Recall the writers of great odes, Milton, Dryden, Pope, Gray, Collins, Wordsworth, Keats, Shelley, Coleridge,—the best they have done will not outstare the "Hound of Heaven." Where shall we find its equal for exaltation of mood that knows no fatigue from the first word to the last? The

motion of angelic hosts must be like the move-
ment of this ode, combining in some marvellous
and mysterious way the swiftness of lightning
with the stately progess of a pageant white with
the blinding white light of an awful Presence.
The note of modernness is the quality which is
most likely to mislead us in forecasting favorably
the durability of contemporary poetry, appealing
as it does to so many personal issues irrelevant
to the standards of immortal art. This is precisely the note which is least conspicuous in the
"Hound of Heaven." The poem might have been
written in the days of Shakespeare, or, in a different speech, by Dante or Calderon. The Rev.
Francis P. LeBuffe, S. J., has written an interesting book on the "Hound of Heaven," pointing out
the analogy between the poem and the psalms of
David; and another Jesuit, the late Rev. J. F. X.
O'Connor, in a published "Study" of the poem,
says that in it Francis Thompson "seems to sing,
in verse, the thought of St. Ignatius in the spiritual exercises,—the thought of St. Paul in the
tender, insistent love of Christ for the soul, and

the yearning of Christ for that soul which ever
runs after creatures, till the love of Christ wakens
in it a love of its God, which dims and deadens
all love of creatures except through love for Him.
This was the love of St. Paul, of St. Ignatius, of
St. Stanislaus, of St. Francis of Assisi, of St.
Clare, of St. Teresa."

The neologisms and archaic words employed in
the poem seem to be a legitimate and instinctive
effort of the poet's inspiration to soar above the
limitations of time and to liberate itself from the
transient accretions of a living, and therefore con-
stantly changing, mode of speech. He strove after
an enfranchisement of utterance, devoid of strati-
fying peculiarities, assignable to no age or epoch,
and understood of all. A soul-shaking thought,
prevalent throughout Christendom, was felt im-
aginatively by a highly endowed poet, and, like
impetuous volcanic fires that fling heavenward
mighty fragments and boulders of mountain in their
red release, found magnificent expression in ele-
mental grandeurs of language, shot through with
the wild lights of hidden flames and transcending

all pettiness of calculated artifice and fugitive fashion.

The dominating idea in the "Hound of Heaven" is so familiar, so—one might say—innate, that it is almost impudent to undertake to explain it. Even in the cases of persons to whom the reading of poetry is an uncultivated and difficult art, there is an instantaneous leap of recognition as the thought emerges from the cloudy glories of the poem. Still, modern popular systems of philosophy are so dehumanizing in their tendencies, and so productive of what may be called secondary and artificially planted instincts, that it is perhaps not entirely useless to attempt to elucidate the obvious.

"The heavens," says Hazlitt, "have gone farther off and become astronomical." The homelike conception of the universe in mediæval times, when dying was like going out of one room into another, and man entertained a neighborly feeling for the angels, has a tendency to disappear as science unfolds more and more new infinities of time and space, new infinities of worlds and forms of life. The curious notion has crept in, that man must sink lower into insignificance with every new discovery of the vastness and huge design of creation. God would seem to have overreached Himself in disclosing His power and majesty, stunning and overwhelming the intellect and heart with the crushing weight of the evidences of His Infinity. We have modern thinkers regarding Christian notions of the Godhead as impossible to a mind acquainted with the paralyzing revelations of scientific knowledge. The late John Fiske used to deride what he called the anthromorphism of the Christian idea of God, as of a venerable, white-bearded man. And these philosophers deem it more reverent to deny any personal relationship between God and man for the reason that God is too great to be interested in man, and man too little to be an object of interest.

Before indicating the essential error of this attitude, it is necessary to state, merely for the sake of historical accuracy, that the Christian conception of the Godhead, as expressed by St. Thomas Aquinas, Dante, Lessius, and a host of Christian writers, has never been approached in its sublime suggestions of Infinite and Eternal power and glory by any modern philosopher. In the second and third Lectures of Cardinal Newman's, "Scope and Nature of University Education," there is an outline of the Christian teaching of the nature of God which, in painstaking accuracy of thought and sheer grandeur of conception, has no counterpart in modern literature.

Let us always remember that telescope and microscope in all the range of their discoveries have not uncovered the existence of anything greater than man himself. The most massive star of the Milky Way is not so wonderful as the smallest human child. Moreover man's present entourage of illimitable space and countless circling suns and planets cannot be said to have cost an omnipotent God more trouble, so to speak, than a universe a million times smaller. The prodigality of the Creator reveals His endless resources; if the vision of sidereal abysses and flaming globes intimidates me and makes me cynical about my unimportance, is it not because I have lost the high consciousness of a spiritual being and forgotten the unplumbed chasms which separate matter from mind?

In Francis Thompson's Catholic philosophy, which must be partially understood if the reader is to get at the heart of the "Hound of Heaven," the tremendous manifestations of God's attributes of power prepare us to expect equally tremendous manifestations of His attributes of love. The more prodigal God is discovered to be in lavish expenditures of omnipotence in the material universe, the more alert the soul becomes to look for and to detect overwhelming surprises of Divine Love. Hence, to Thompson there was nothing irrational in the special revelation of God to man, in His Incarnation, His death on the cross, and His sacramental life in the Church. The Divine energy of God's love, as displayed in the supernatural revelation of Himself, seems to be even vaster and more intense than the Divine energy of creation displayed in the revelation of nature. Every new revelation of God's power and wisdom which science unfolds serves only to restore a balance in our mind between God's power and God's love. The more astronomical the heavens become, the closer they bring God to us.

Another conception of God to be kept in mind, if we are to grasp the meaning of the "Hound of Heaven," is the omniscient character, the infinite perfection, of God's knowledge. God sees each of us as fully and completely as if there were no one else and nothing else to see except us. Practically speaking, God gives each one of us His undivided attention. And through this spacious channel of His Divine and exclusive attention pour the ocean-tides of His love. The weak soul is afraid of the terrible excess of Divine Love. It tries to elude it; but Love meets it at every cross-road and by-path, down which it would run and hide itself, and gently turns it back.

Francis Thompson, in an interpretation of "A Narrow Vessel," has left us in prose a description of human weakness and wilfulness reluctant of its true bliss. The following passage is an excellent commentary on the "Hound of Heaven."

38

"Though God," he says, "asks of the soul but to love Him what it may, and is ready to give an increased love for a poor little, the soul feels that this infinite love demands naturally its whole self, that if it begin to love God it may not stop short of all it has to yield. It is troubled, even if it did go a brief way, on the upward path; it fears and recoils from the whole great surrender, the constant effort beyond itself which is sensibly laid on it. It falls back with relieved contentment on some human love, a love on its own plane, where somewhat short of total surrender may go to requital, where no upward effort is needful. And it ends by giving for the meanest, the most unsufficing and half-hearted return, that utter self-surrender and self-effacement which it denied to God. Even (how rarely) if the return be such as mortal may render, how empty and unsatiated it leaves the soul. One always is less generous to love than the other."

God walks morning, noon and eve in the garden of the soul, calling it to a happiness which affrights it. And the timid and self-seeking soul strives to hide itself under the stars, under the clouds of heaven, under human love, under the distractions of work and pleasure and study, offers itself as a wistful servitor to child and man and nature, if they will but afford it a refuge from the persistent and gentle accents of pursuivant Love. But all things are in league with God, Who made and rules them. They cannot conspire against Him. They betray the refugee. He turns in abject surrender, and is astonished to find the rest and happiness that he quested for so wildly. The Divine thwartings which had harassed the soul become a tender mystery of Infinite Love forcing itself upon an unworthy and unwilling creature. Someone has said that every life is a romance of Divine Love. The "Hound of Heaven" is a version of that romance which smites the soul into an humble mood of acknowledgment and penitence.

JAMES J. DALY, S. J.

OF "THE HOUND OF HEAVEN"

RANCIS THOMPSON, born in Preston in 1859, spent the greater part of his mature life in London where he died in 1907. He was educated at Ushaw College near Durham, and afterwards went to Owens College, Manchester, to qualify as a doctor.

But his gift as prescriber and healer lay elsewhere than in the consulting-room. He walked to London in search of a living, finding, indeed, a prolonged near approach to death in its streets; until at length his literary powers were discovered by himself and by others, and he began, in his later twenties, an outpouring of verse which endured for a half-decade of years—his "Poems," his "Sister Songs," and his "New Poems."

"The Hound of Heaven" "marked the return of

the nineteenth century to Thomas à Kempis." The
great poetry of it transcended, in itself and in its
influence, all conventions; so that it won the love
of a Catholic Mystic like Coventry Patmore; was
included by Dean Beeching in his "Lyra Sacra"
among its older high compeers; and gave new heart
to quite another manner of man, Edward Burne-
Jones.

W. M.

THE HOUND OF HEAVEN

I FLED Him, down the nights and
     down the days;
    I fled Him, down the arches of the
     years;
I fled Him, down the labyrinthine ways
  Of my own mind; and in the mist of tears
I hid from Him, and under running laughter.
     Up vistaed hopes, I sped;
     And shot, precipitated,
Adown Titanic glooms of chasmèd fears,
  From those strong Feet that followed, followed
    after.

     But with unhurrying chase,
     And unperturbèd pace,
Deliberate speed, majestic instancy,
    They beat—and a Voice beat
    More instant than the Feet—
"All things betray thee, who betrayest Me."

THE HOUND OF HEAVEN

I pleaded, out law-wise,
By many a hearted casement, curtained red,
  Trellised with intertwining charities
(For, though I knew His love Who followèd,
    Yet was I sore adread
Lest, having Him, I must have naught beside);
But, if one little casement parted wide,
  The gust of His approach would clash it to.
  Fear wist not to evade as Love wist to pursue.
Across the margent of the world I fled,
  And troubled the gold gateways of the stars,
  Smiting for shelter on their clangèd bars;
    Fretted to dulcet jars
And silvern chatter the pale ports o' the moon.
I said to dawn: Be sudden; to eve: Be soon—
  With thy young skyey blossoms heap me over
    From this tremendous Lover!
Float thy vague veil about me, lest He see!
  I tempted all His servitors, but to find
My own betrayal in their constancy,
In faith to Him their fickleness to me,
  Their traitorous trueness, and their loyal deceit.
To all swift things for swiftness did I sue;

THE HOUND OF HEAVEN

Clung to the whistling mane of every wind.
But whether they swept, smoothly fleet,
The long savannahs of the blue;
Or whether, Thunder-driven,
They clanged His chariot 'thwart a heaven
Plashy with flying lightnings round the spurn o'
their feet:—
Fear wist not to evade as Love wist to pursue.

Still with unhurrying chase,
And unperturbèd pace,
Deliberate speed, majestic instancy,
Came on the following Feet,
And a Voice above their beat—
"Naught shelters thee, who wilt not shelter Me."

I SOUGHT no more that after which I
        strayed
      In face of man or maid;
      But still within the little children's
      eyes
      Seems something, something that replies,
They at least are for me, surely for me!
I turned me to them very wistfully;
But just as their young eyes grew sudden fair
      With dawning answers there,
Their angel plucked them from me by the hair.

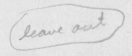

OME then, ye other children,
  Nature's—share
  With me" (said I) "your delicate
   fellowship;
Let me greet you lip to lip,
Let me twine with you caresses,
  Wantoning
With our Lady-Mother's vagrant tresses,
  Banqueting
With her in her wind-walled palace,
Underneath her azured daïs,
Quaffing, as your taintless way is,
  From a chalice
Lucent-weeping out of the dayspring."
  So it was done:
I in their delicate fellowship was one—
Drew the bolt of Nature's secrecies.
  I knew all the swift importings
  On the wilful face of skies;
  I knew how the clouds arise,

THE HOUND OF HEAVEN

Spumèd of the wild sea-snortings;
All that's born or dies
Rose and drooped with;   made them shapers
Of mine own moods, or wailful or divine—
With them joyed and was bereaven.
I was heavy with the even,
When she lit her glimmering tapers
Round the day's dead sanctities.
I laughed in the morning's eyes.
I triumphed and I saddened with all weather,
Heaven and I wept together,
And its sweet tears were salt with mortal mine;
Against the red throb of its sunset-heart
I laid my own to beat,
And share commingling heat;
But not by that, by that, was eased my human
smart.
In vain my tears were wet on Heaven's grey cheek.
For ah! we know not what each other says,
These things and I; in sound *I* speak—
Their sound is but their stir, they speak by silences.
Nature, poor stepdame, cannot slake by drouth;
Let her, if she would owe me,

THE HOUND OF HEAVEN

Drop yon blue bosom-veil of sky, and show me
  The breasts o' her tenderness:
Never did any milk of hers once bless
  My thirsting mouth.
  Nigh and nigh draws the chase,
   With unperturbèd pace,
  Deliberate speed, majestic instancy,
   And past those noisèd Feet
   A Voice comes yet more fleet—
  "Lo! naught contents thee, who content'st
  not Me."

NAKED I wait Thy love's uplifted
stroke!
My harness piece by piece Thou
hast hewn from me,
And smitten me to my knee;
I am defenceless utterly.
I slept, methinks, and woke,
And, slowly gazing, find me stripped in sleep.
In the rash lustihead of my young powers,
I shook the pillaring hours
And pulled my life upon me; grimed with smears,
I stand amid the dust o' the mounded years—
My mangled youth lies dead beneath the heap.
My days have crackled and gone up in smoke,
Have puffed and burst as sun-starts on a stream.
Yea, faileth now even dream
The dreamer, and the lute the lutanist;
Even the linked fantasies, in whose blossomy twist
I swung the earth a trinket at my wrist,
Are yielding; cords of all too weak account

For earth, with heavy griefs so overplussed.
      Ah! is Thy love indeed
A weed, albeit an amaranthine weed,
Suffering no flowers except its own to mount?
          Ah! must—
          Designer infinite!—
Ah! must Thou char the wood ere Thou canst
          limn with it?
My freshness spent its wavering shower i' the dust;
And now my heart is as a broken fount,
Wherein tear-drippings stagnate, spilt down ever
          From the dank thoughts that shiver
Upon the sighful branches of my mind.
          Such is; what is to be?
The pulp so bitter, how shall taste the rind?
I dimly guess what Time in mists confounds;
Yet ever and anon a trumpet sounds
From the hid battlements of Eternity:
Those shaken mists a space unsettle, then
Round the half-glimpsèd turrets slowly wash
          again;
          But not ere him who summoneth
          I first have seen, enwound

56

THE HOUND OF HEAVEN

With glooming robes purpureal, cypress-crowned;
His name I know, and what his trumpet saith.
Whether man's heart or life it be which yields
  Thee harvest, must Thy harvest fields
  Be dunged with rotten death?

NOW of that long pursuit
    Comes on at hand the bruit;
    That Voice is round me like a
        bursting sea:
  "And is thy earth so marred,
    Shattered in shard on shard?
Lo, all things fly thee, for thou fliest Me!
    Strange, piteous, futile thing,
Wherefore should any set thee love apart?
Seeing none but I makes much of naught" (He
    said),
"And human love needs human meriting:
    How hast thou merited—
Of all man's clotted clay the dingiest clot?
    Alack, thou knowest not
How little worthy of any love thou art!
Whom wilt thou find to love ignoble thee,
    Save Me, save only Me?
All which I took from thee I did but take,
    Not for thy harms,

But just that thou might'st seek it in My arms.
　　　All which thy child's mistake
Fancies as lost, I have stored for thee at home:
　　　Rise, clasp My hand, and come."

　　　Halts by me that footfall:
　　　Is my gloom, after all,
Shade of His hand, outstretched caressingly?
　　　"Ah, fondest, blindest, weakest,
　　　I am He Whom thou seekest!
Thou dravest love from thee, who dravest Me."